The Day I Met Diana, Princess of Wales

The Day I Met Diana, Princess of Wales

THE PEOPLE'S STORIES

LONG BARN BOOKS

PUBLISHED BY
LONG BARN BOOKS

Ebrington, Gloucestershire GL55 6NW

First published 1997
1 3 5 7 9 10 8 6 4 2

Set in 12/14.5pt Monotype Garamond
Printed and bound by Redwood Books, Trowbridge, Wiltshire

ISBN 0 952 8285 9 6

Preface

The contributions to this book came from replies to a request published in the national and regional media for stories about individual meetings over the years with Diana, Princess of Wales. They have been chosen from the very many sent in, after careful reading and thought, not only for themselves but because they all in some way stand as representatives of dozens of other, similar stories.

Some meetings with the Princess were public, others very private, some were formal, many not. Together, they make up a vivid portrait of Diana.

They reveal her as generous with her time, and unhurried with people who wanted to tell things to her; as unstuffy, and with a sure knack of taking any edginess or uncertainty out of an occasion and putting anxious people at their ease. They reveal someone who laughed a great deal – the word often used is 'giggled' – and made others do so; time and again the phrase 'her infectious laugh' jumped from the pages of the letters. They reveal what an impact her beauty made on everyone – her height, her slimness – at times, a worrying thin-ness

– her flawless skin and above all, as her brother Earl Spencer said in his address at her funeral 'those unforgettable blue eyes.'

Her warmth, her sparkle, her enthusiasm, her presence – an aura, – a magic. All this is here. Her loving and utterly genuine concern for people, and her need to be with those who were ill or in some way in distress, with the disfigured, disabled and disadvantaged, shines out. As one writer puts it, she took time and trouble over those whom many 'would not pass the time of day with'. Of course a large number of her visits to hospitals and hospices were official and public, but very many were not. The hours spent sitting at bedsides – and on beds – the surprise telephone calls and trips to the homes and hospital rooms of people who needed and had appealed to her were unknown to the media. So many of the letters sent give the lie to criticism that 'she only did it for effect – for publicity – for attention – for the cameras.'

Perhaps her passion for being with, and trying to bring comfort to, those in various kinds of need and distress, came from a corresponding need within her, some sense of her own inadequacy that wanted reassurance. If so, does it matter? How many people do good out of the purest and most disinterested motives? Diana knew what she meant to people and the importance of what only she could give to them. It was what she did and the effect it had that counted. As the Queen said in her televised tribute, 'Diana made very, very many people happy.'

Everyone has been most generous in offering their stories about her for publication and in revealing their very personal thoughts and feelings. Many wanted to remain anonymous. I think that all wrote for two reasons: to pay tribute to and give thanks for the life, work and person of Diana, and as their own way of contributing to the funds in her name.

Reading the letters has been a fascinating and a moving experience. Millions of words have been written about Diana, and doubtless millions more will be, but these words are spontaneous and heartfelt, from ordinary people of many ages and kinds, who met her at various stages through her life and perhaps because they 'speak as they found' they are some of the most valuable.

This book is not intended to be part of any movement to canonize the memory of Diana. It has been written by people who were touched by her and came to love her, the same kind of people who, perhaps to their own surprise, found themselves taking flowers to the Royal Palaces, lining the streets for her funeral, queuing for hours to sign the books of condolence, keeping candlelit vigils in the parks and sharing in that astonishing one minute of silence. But they do not think of her as a saint or an angel, with-out fault or blemish, they recognize her as simply a human being – 'like one of us' as so many letter writers put it.

Yet part of the point is that she was not quite like one of us. She became Royal – whatever that means – and so took on the aura of Royalty. It was this combination, of being set apart and somehow special while still remaining in touch and in tune with the everyday lives and needs of people that was one of the secrets of her astonishing appeal. After her divorce I read that she was 'no longer untouchable.' But even at her most glamorous and Princess-ly, Diana had never been that.

Reading and selecting from these letters has been a fascinating and most moving experience – perhaps surprisingly, for someone who has never been a Royalist. Cynical commentators referred to the mass hysteria abroad at the time of Diana's death, but what I felt then, along with millions of others, was simply genuine shock, grief and distress at the loss of such a remarkable young woman, followed almost immediately by a desire to acknowledge, and in some way continue, the work that she did.

The idea for this book came from my 12-year old daughter who instinctively recognized that at the time of a shocking death people feel the need both to say something and to do something. Giving to the charities supported by Diana, Princess of Wales is the way for most of us and all proceeds from this book will go to the Landmines Removal Programme and the Diana, Princess of Wales Memorial Fund.

I have a story of my own of 'the day I met Diana.' It is quite brief and unremarkable but what she said to me seems important. I had had an extremely busy day in London, it was a hot afternoon, and at the end of it, I remembered that I had to provide supper for my family at home in Gloucestershire and that the cupboard there was bare. After seeing a publisher in Kensington, I dashed down into the food hall of Marks and Spencer in the High Street to grab some supplies before catching the train home. Fresh prawns, mayonnaise, salad and French bread seemed quick and easy, but as I reached the seafood counter I saw that there was just one remaining pack of shell-on prawns. I reached for them at exactly the moment as another hand touched the packet. Our hands met on that fish and I was furious, hot, tired ... I glared up ... and into 'those unforgettable blue eyes.' There was Diana, in jeans and shirt, smiling with amusement but apologetically, looking stunning and making me immediately conscious of my own hot and bothered state.

Why do we respond as we do to Royalty, often in spite of ourselves? I dropped the packet of prawns as if they were red hot, yielding all claim to them at once, mumbling something ... whereupon Diana simply picked them up and dropped them into my basket. 'No,' she said, tucking them away under the salad, 'I'm sure your need is greater than mine.'

As someone commented, those words could stand as an epitaph for much of Diana's life and work – and at any rate, as the sub-title of this book.

Lady about to be presented to H.R.H. the Princess of Wales: 'Should I curtsy, Ma'am?'
Diana: 'I suppose so – silly isn't it?'

رک

When Princess Diana was five and lived at Park House on the Sandringham estate, I used to do a spot of secretarial work for her father, Lord Althorp.

One evening there was a heck of a noise – it was Diana stomping down the stone-flagged entrance hall in her mother's metal-tipped stiletto heeled shoes; then she marched into the library-cum-office. She was immediately ordered out by her father.

Her impish nature was apparent, even at that early age, for she immediately re-opened the door, cheekily peeped round, then hurried back to the drawing room – making more noise than ever.

LESLIE M. COWDEN, Stoke on Trent

✌

I met Diana when she was fourteen and not when she was Princess of Wales. It was in Ibiza in August 1975. My sister was nanny to an Admiral's two children and I joined her for two weeks holiday. Diana, her mother, brother and one sister, who were friends of the family joined them for a week at the same time.

One afternoon, Diana and I hired a pedallo from a local beach. We had pedalled out a fair distance when we realized that the pedallo was filling up with water and starting to sink. Luckily the water was fairly shallow so we held our cameras, hats, etc. above our heads and waded ashore with a lot of giggles and surreptitious looks around to see if anyone could see us. We were so worried that we would be told or made to pay for the pedallo which had sunk. But when we got to the beach we ran as fast as we could back to our villa. We never owned up or went back to the same place.

SOPHIE AMES, Ashtead, Surrey.

I met Lady Diana Spencer on the Royal Yacht at Cowes Week in August 1980. I was 17, and Prince Charles and Prince Edward were hosting the evening – I had gone as the partner of the friend of a friend.

There were fourteen of us for dinner and then a little party afterwards, on the deck, until about 2 a.m. It was fantastic! At one stage in the evening I wanted to go to the loo, and looking around at the people there, obviously thought that Diana was the most approachable, as she was a girl almost of my own age, and asked her if she could show me the way. Instead she said, 'Come with me to my cabin.'

'You have a cabin?'

'Yes, my family and I have stayed a few times on Britannia,' she said matter-of-factly and not at all in the snooty way one might have expected.

I followed her down to her very comfortable cabin, and we pottered around for a bit, checking our make-up, brushing our hair and so on, and I remember thinking that she was just like me – similar age, similar clothes and we wore the same make-up too, with that metallic bright blue eye-liner everyone used in the '80s. She was so friendly and she had never met me before, and had no reason to make such an effort, take me to her own cabin and share her things with me. I felt very comfortable with her.

At the party she danced the tango with Prince Edward and was so full of energy, but she did not seem to be with Prince Charles at all that evening, and when the papers were full of rumours about them a few weeks later, I told my mother there was nothing in it. 'They didn't even dance together that evening!' I said.

I feel so privileged to have met her, and in such informal and private circumstances. I took little interest in her royal role, and I was taken aback by how deeply saddened I felt by her untimely death.

MRS JANE DUCKWORTH, London W3

و

Until Wve years ago I worked in a bank near the Oxford Street end of Baker Street, convenient for Selfridges' store, where more often than not I would spend my lunch hour browsing. I always used the Orchard Street entrance next to the food hall and quite often an elderly blind man would be standing at this entrance, not quite on the pavement but tucked just inside to shelter from the weather. He was selling matches from a tray supported by a sling around his neck.

Not long after the announcement of the engagement of Charles and Diana and whilst the picture of the happy couple walking in the gardens of Buckingham Palace was still fresh in our minds, I happened to be in Selfridges' hurrying towards this exit behind a tall, slim young woman also striding out in the same direction. When we were almost outside, she suddenly came to a halt in front of the blind man, forcing me to pull up quickly to avoid colliding with her. Passing her, slightly annoyed, I was about to glare at her when I was taken aback to see who she was and what she was doing.

Without a word, Lady Diana, as she then was, had reached inside her handbag and taken out her purse and was placing something into the tray of the blind man. As he thanked her she walked away towards the busy street of shoppers, having taken no matches in return. There were no photographers or journalists to record the event. She was just a lone woman on a shopping expedition. If only her life could have remained that simple.

MRS ANN MOUKAYED, London, SW14

༄

I cannot believe that sixteen years ago I was more than ready to get off a train and turn around to go home, back to a tearful wife and three year old daughter. I was in no mood for leaving them for the next six months, though I knew all along that there would be plenty of people in the world who would have given their right arms to have taken my place. And it hardly seems possible to me now that I could have contemplated not wanting to go on a journey that was to be such a wonderful experience and would become so memorable. Let's face it, not many people went on honeymoon with the future King and Queen of England.

I had a marvellous time with the Royal couple. The shy bride was an absolute delight to us all on board, full of fun and radiating happiness – even though there were 240 of us to share her days. Our spirits were indeed lifted by this delightful lady, so that the six months ahead seemed bearable after all.

During the cruise all the crew were introduced to the Princess, and even then she had the knack of making you feel so completely at ease, chatting to everyone. We talked about where I had trained as a chef, and the wedding cake that had accompanied them on board. She was also anxious to know if we were enjoying the cruise as much as Prince Charles and she were.

I feel proud and privileged to have been on that voyage and to have been part of a extremely happy time in Diana's life.

ANDREW D'ARCY, Leading Cook,
Royal Yacht Britannia 1980-1983

🙠

I am an ex-ATS and I have been to several 'not forgotten' garden parties at Buckingham Palace. The most memorable was 1981, the Year of the Disabled, when the Prince of Wales and Diana came along and spoke to me and to my carer. We asked to see her engagement ring which she showed to us. She then said, 'The people up the other end told me that they are selling these rings in Woolworth's for twenty six pounds.' Then she turned and said to Prince Charles, 'Look what you could have saved!' – and to us, 'Perhaps we ought to buy one of those in case I lose this.'

MISS D. L. WHITMARSH, Dovercourt, Essex

ॐ

I met Princess Diana in November 1981 on her own first official opening ceremony since becoming the Princess of Wales. She had come to open the new Northampton Head Post Office and all postmen with children under the age of twelve had been asked to put their children's names forward so that a group of about 15 could be picked to meet her. I was eleven at the time and was very lucky to be chosen. I picked some roses from our own garden and wrapped the stems in foil, but by the time Princess Diana reached us my roses were beginning to droop! I was on the end of the row and one of the last to meet her. When she reached me she said, 'Are those flowers for me?' and gave me a lovely smile. She then smelt them and said, 'Are they from your garden? I love the smell of Northamptonshire roses.'

She was a very genuine and caring person and I like to think she appreciated my drooping roses in foil as much as any of the proper posies she had received, by the lovely smile that she gave me.

MISS AMANDA GEORGE, Moulton, Northampton

My wife and I met Diana, Princess of Wales, in 1983 on one of her first solo public engagements. At one point she turned to the Lord Lieutenant and whispered, 'What do I do next?'

I told her that she had given much joy to many people that day and she thanked me and then added to my wife, 'But I wish I had more time to visit your wonderful shoe shops!'

MR AND MRS TONY BOOTLE, Aylesbury, Bucks

ॐ

On 2 May 1984, the Royal Warrant Holders Association held a reception at the Hilton Hotel, Park Lane, for its members to meet the Prince and Princess of Wales. Several hundred people were present and we were divided into groups of about ten down each side of the Hilton ballroom – the Prince moved along one side and my husband and I were among those to meet the Princess on the other.

Before she reached us, we watched as she talked for a minute or two to each of the fifty or so people who preceded us.

When eventually I was presented to Princess Diana as the managing director of Halcyon Days, without a moment's hesitation she said 'Oh, I simply love your shop and we had such marvellous wedding presents that came from there – the Duchess of Kent gave us an adorable tiny carriage clock with enamelled flowers and ...' She reeled off precise descriptions of four other gifts she and the Prince of Wales had received from Halcyon Days, saying who had given each one of them, ending with: '... and my husband gave me the sweetest enamel box with a very romantic message.' She then turned to speak to my husband who was all but overwhelmed by the beauty of those wonderful aquamarine eyes as he gazed into them.

After she had moved on we realized how astonishing it was that among a crowd of people, all of whom undoubtedly must have discussed with her their individual connections with the Royal Family, she had summoned up so accurately five of the many thousands of wedding presents received almost three years earlier.

MRS SUSAN BENJAMIN, London, W1

෴

My meeting with Diana was brief but unforgettable. It was a sunny, but cold November morning in 1984 when my family and I went down to Southampton, after receiving an invitation from P & O to attend the ceremony of naming a new cruise liner, 'Royal Princess'. I watched and listened to the ceremony which was taking place on a rostrum at the far end of the ship, never imagining that she would reach our viewing spot during her walkabout. But it was a great thrill when she came over to me and shook hands. Her Wrst words were to say how sorry she was that we had been standing in the cold for so long, and that we should have carried a little bottle of whisky in our handbags. The funny thing was that I did have one in my bag in anticipation of a long wait to see this beautiful young lady – only I lacked the courage to say so!

MRS BETTY LETTRES, Shoreham by Sea, Sussex

ॐ

It was a cold, damp November day about three years ago when I dashed up the steps leading to the West Yorkshire Playhouse in Leeds for a lunch appointment with a friend. I was confronted by a huge crowd and thought that if I could push my way to the front and explain to a policeman on duty that I just wanted to reach the dining room, he would let me through. 'No way,' he said, holding up a large hand. I then noticed a line of dignitaries and actors assembling and a limousine drawing up at the entrance. A young girl who looked about the same age as one of my daughters got out and started to chat to the chosen few. Just as it was beginning to dawn upon me who she was, she left the line-up and walked directly to where I was standing.

'Hullo,' she said. 'You look so cold, have you been waiting long?' She genuinely cared about it – that much was written in her eyes. There was no way that I could tell her the truth – that I had not come there specially to see her. I mumbled that I was fine, thank you.

She gave me a smile that warmed me for the rest of the week.

MRS PAMELA PENNOCK, Colton Village, Leeds

༜

I met Princess Diana when she came to visit Carlisle, 30 miles from the village where I live. My friend and I, together with our two daughters, stood among others lining the street waiting for the walkabout. Luckily, the Princess came along our side. Shaking my friend's and her daughter's hand and then my own, she turned to go forwards towards the waiting car. Unthinkingly, I shouted out 'Oh! Diana'. She, like a normal everyday person, looked quickly round and I said 'You've missed my daughter.' She immediately came back, took my daughter's hand between both her own, and apologized for missing her out. I shall never forget how lovely that was of her and afterwards I realized the enormity of what I'd done by just shouting out 'Oh! Diana.' It had made no difference. She was like one of us.

MRS M. FRAZER, Maryport, Cumbria

ॐ

I would like to relate on the day my mother, Mrs Bottomley, met Diana, Princess of Wales. It was March '82 at the Albany in Deptford, of which the Princess of Wales was then Patron

We had all been waiting in the crowd to see her arrive, which we did and then she went into Albany. On leaving, however, she came into the crowd and seemed to head towards us. My mother was at the front and my stepfather and I a little way back. The Princess of Wales took my mother's hand and thanked her for waiting so long and hoped my mother hadn't neglected her husband in not getting his dinner. My mother replied that it didn't matter as they were only having sausages that day. The Princess really laughed!

MS DIANE HUMPHRYS, London, SE12

J oseph Arnold (Card Printing), Church, Lancashire, and a new factory building, to be opened by Diana, Princess of Wales. My son worked there, as a trainee estimator, and so managed to provide one invitation to greet her on one of her first solo engagements.

The day was fine, the roped-off crowds in the large car park were considerable, and we had to be patient, until the factory was duly toured and opened.

The first glimpse of the Princess as she emerged from her car was rather blocked by large security men but we soon saw her more closely, in a red and white outfit, very smart and bright as she moved over to the long 4-deep lines of people, smiling and completely ignoring the anxiety of her minders, anxious to ensure that her schedule was slick and quick. She took proffered hands, thanked people for good wishes, and answered enquiries about her infant son, William, with true maternal pride. I overheard her say, on seeing a pushchair, that she needed one of those, which gave us a warm image of her baby outgrowing his pram.

She was a picture of health, eyes clear and glowing, as she passed along. She stopped when she saw a camera, so that we could get our own personal pictures – a much appreciated consideration. She was an arm's reach away as I aimed my camera – her eyes were impressed forever on my mind – deep, deep blue, so special. I was dumbfounded by it all. She clearly enjoyed it too, though it was so much work. Then,

Preston Hospital awaited, and she was whisked away.

A large lady, elderly and lame, was met by her son, and as she leaned upon him to leave, she kept repeating, 'Ooh, Jack, she was so lovely, I shall never forget Jack, she was beautiful, she was so nice, Jack. I feel it were a privilege, Jack.'

I thought then, how marvellous for that lady to be so happy; and everyone else was murmuring and chatting with strangers, a happy band of smiling folk, and all because of one young woman.

MRS ELLA TOWNLEY, Blackburn, Lancashire

ॐ

I met Princess Diana in Glasgow when she opened a Child Line Centre with Esther Rantzen. The roads were blocked off and crowds of factory girls were standing; they didn't want to miss seeing her so they sent for bags of chips which they stood eating. The princess came out of the building and they all pushed out their hands (smelling of vinegar). Then they said, 'What about this wee woman (I am small), she has been waiting two hours to take your photo.' So, she stopped in front of me, then shook my hand. I can still feel the warm, firm hand grasp and the lovely smile. No limp, hardly touching handshake, but one that would have held me up if I had fallen.

MRS J. S. CLARKSON, Lanark, Scotland

༃

The first time I met Princess Diana was when she came to Preston in 1990. I was standing in the crowd waiting for her. In front of us was a border of rose bushes and then the path that the princess was to walk down. But when she arrived she saw the crowd and ploughed straight through the bushes towards us, laddering her tights on the way.

The second time I met her was in Blackpool in 1992. She was visiting an old people's home and again I was waiting in a crowd outside, hoping to see her. But just before she came out it started to rain, so that everyone was saying that she wouldn't do a walkabout now. But when she came out of the home she came straight across to us in the pouring rain, this time ploughing through long wet grass on the way. She did not even have an umbrella and she got soaked. She really was the people's princess.

MISS RITA SHARPLES, Longton, Nr. Preston, Lancashire

I shook hands with Diana about ten years ago when I worked at a mental hospital, Harperbury, in St Alban's. I was a Nursing Assistant in the day care units and we used to take the residents out as often as we could, so when the local paper announced that she was going to open the new shopping centre, it was an opportunity not to be missed to get out for half a day.

It sounds awful but the first thing that struck me about her were her big feet. It was in the days when she still wore flat shoes so as not to tower over Prince Charles. And she walked like a ballerina with her feet at 45 degrees. I was determined not to make a fuss as some other people were doing, but as she got nearer I had an overwhelming urge to put my hand out and try and shake hers. She laughed because I was wearing a pair of big parrot ear-rings and she looked at me as if I were the only person there.

MRS RACHEL ELLAM-LLOYD,
Greenford, Middlesex

مص

Armed with camera, drink and sandwiches, I set out for Inverness town centre. A visit by Diana, Princess of Wales was my quest.

I managed to get a pole position in front of the Town House and perched my camera on a tall, metal litterbin in anticipation of getting a good photograph.

The Princess came into view led by her personal detective. I moved the camera to get a better picture and to my horror and embarrassment the batteries fell out of the camera and rolled into the gutter. Thinking it might be something sinister the detective dashed forward, but realizing my predicament, Diana laughed and said, 'I'll stand here until you fix it.' There was plenty of advice offered, even from the chief inspector of police, camera repaired after much laughter, and instamatic finally completed its task.

Returning home, still in jubilant mood and laughing to myself I then took our elderly dog for a walk. As I turned the corner a maroon Rolls Royce came into view and I realized that it was Diana on her way back to the airport. She was still smiling and waving – a moment I cherish, just me and my dog, saying a personal farewell.

MRS J. ROBINSON, Balloch, by Inverness, Scotland

During 1990 Princess Diana opened a building in Brighton for the blind and partially sighted. My grandson, who was four at the time, is partially sighted and was taken by his mother to the opening on the afternoon of that day.

During the morning Diana attended a conference at the Brighton Centre and I thought it would be nice to see her. As she passed me on her way out I said 'You will be seeing my little grandson this afternoon.' She took my hand in hers and said 'What's his name?', to which I replied, 'Daniel.' That evening she was on television talking to him. I felt so happy, she had a warmth about her that you could not describe. Everything that has been said about her is true. She made you feel special and I shall never forget her.

ANONYMOUS CONTRIBUTOR, Brighton, Sussex

ॐ

It was a cold December morning in 1992 and getting on for nine o'clock. My almost two-month old son, Adam, was tucked up in his pram and he and I were ready for our usual walk along Whitley Bay sea front, going towards Cullercoats.

With the sea almost in view, I noticed that there were a few police officers about and barriers being set up at the side of the road, and asked a woman who was watching what was happening. She told me that the Princess of Wales was visiting the 'Turning Point Project' across the road from where we were standing, at eleven o'clock.

Should I stay and see her, or carry on with my usual walk? But I could do that any day and a chance like this did not come very often. I stayed. Adam was fast asleep and would be for a good while, and I knew that he would be quite warm enough, tucked into his pram.

The time went on, and a crowd gathered; the air was filled with excitement – people chatted to one another as if they had been friends for years! A girl standing next to me showed me her bandaged right hand – she had just been to have some stitches examined at the doctor's and I could tell she was concerned that if the Princess shook her hand, it would have to be the left one. I assured her that I felt Diana would not mind that in the least and she told me that I must get Adam out of his pram when she did her walkabout, as the Princess was known to love babies and would be certain to come across.

Policemen and women chatted to the people. I had not realized that they had to face the crowd the whole time and could not look at the Princess, for security reasons. Meanwhile, the security officers talked to each other, looking round all the time.

Then two cars arrived and the people went crazy, shouting Diana's name. She got out of her car and waved and smiled at us all. The Princess was more beautiful than I had ever imagined, so stunning and elegant I think really I felt as if I was dreaming this day. Wearing a navy blue pleated skirt with a three-quarter jacket, she was style itself that day. A visit like this really showed her caring side, too, for people who others would not even pass the time of day with.

Princess Diana went on into the house, shaking hands with the people who managed the project and accepting a bouquet of flowers. Her meeting there was to last about twenty minutes, followed by the walkabout.

Photographers had positioned themselves on ladders and walls, preparing to take lots of photographs, and reporters were making notes. Everyone chattered excitedly and children, some up on fathers' shoulders, shouted for Diana.

Eventually, she came out and the walkabout began. The young girl next to me said that Adam, who had only woken up a few moments before, must be on view, so out he came. I sat him on the barrier, obviously having a very tight hold of him!

Diana was receiving single roses and bunches of flowers everywhere, so many that she could not carry them. I could feel my whole body shaking with sheer excitement and nervousness, which I hoped would not get the better of me if Diana stopped to speak.

And then there she was, actually in front of Adam and me. She spoke directly to him, smiling her beautiful smile. 'Who's wrapped up nice and warm then,' she said, with a caring, mother's voice. She smiled right at me and then moved on. My legs were total jelly. I could not believe that I had actually met Princess Diana, and that she had spoken to my baby!

I could see that her car door was open and ready and it was time for this remarkable lady to go. Her smile and her blue eyes shone out at everyone as she gave a final wave, the car door shut – and it was all over.

Then, it was back to life as normal. People were saying their good-byes. I tucked Adam up in his pram. I was far too excited for our walk now, and headed home.

A week later, our local paper had a display board full of photographs taken of the Princess's visit and to my delight, there was Adam in his snow suit, sitting on the barrier, with Diana just two people away from us.

Adam, who is almost five, loved Princess Diana very much and he continues to ask questions about her life and her shocking death. It was he who broke the news. He said in his most grown-up voice, 'Diana of Wales has died in a car crash.' I remember staring at the television, listening to the news, and that I could not seem to grasp what they were saying. I do not think that I will ever get over her death. The world will still be mourning one of the most caring of people ever, for a very long time to come.

MRS DIANA BURNS, Newcastle upon Tyne

ॐ

My own recollection dates from 7 November 1995, when Princess Diana came to Liverpool to open the new Women's Hospital, and to visit a new housing project. In between these two appointments, she visited Liverpool Cathedral and I, along with many others, waited for her to leave.

Eventually she emerged, and came over to us. I was the first person to shake her hand, and I told her I had tried to see her on several occasions, but had only ever managed to see the back of her head! She gave that lovely smile, went to move on, then shouted back over her shoulder, 'That's the best bit!'

COLIN TURNOCK, Liverpool

჻

In 1993 my 100-year old aunt was invited to a garden party at Buckingham Palace and I was also invited to push her wheelchair.

On the day, I pushed her to the front of the lines of waiting guests saying 'My aunt is 100' as we went. People seemed happy to make way for her. An equerry had heard me and came up and said that Princess Diana would speak to my aunt.

Half an hour later the Princess arrived and the equerry introduced my aunt Bengie, Miss Forbes-Dunlop. Aunt B. had obviously been rehearsing what she wanted to say to the Princess. Princess Diana bent over the frail old lady and took her hand, saying a few words of encouragement. All Aunt Bengie's carefully rehearsed words poured out. To my horror, she talked non-stop for fully five minutes and the Princess just stood there smiling. With amazing patience she never interrupted, but let the old lady continue until at last the words dried up. Then Princess Diana straightened up and gave me a beaming smile, said a few more words and was gone.

Aunt Bengie died peacefully nine months later, bright to the end. She never tired of telling people how she met Princess Diana and how the Princess spoke to her for over five minutes at the garden party.

MRS ANGELA KELLIE, Evanton,
Ross-shire, Scotland

To commemorate the 150th anniversary of the Northern Counties School for the Deaf, Princess Diana paid a visit. She was told that in the nursery department a group of deaf mothers with deaf and hearing toddlers would be attending their weekly get-together. The Princess asked if she might call in to see them. I shall always cherish this memory, as she conversed in sign language with every mother, asking questions such as 'How do you know if your baby is crying in the night?' During one conversation with a mother she was asked about the two princes and she replied in sign language that William was a naughty boy. It was just 'mum to mum' conversation.

MRS L. AVISON, North Heaton, Newcastle upon Tyne

࿐

In February 1990, the Beach Road at Prestatyn was flooded by the sea, engulfing my home and many other houses. Several victims of this disaster were invited to meet the Princess of Wales at Towyn Community Centre for her to cheer our spirits and temporarily forget the trauma of being flooded out of our homes. We stood around drinking tea, eating cakes, etc. while Princess Diana, our Princess of Wales, joined in and chatted with us all, with warmth and sincerity. After spending some time with us, she left and got into her car. I stood near her and when she saw me, she wound down her window. 'Now you can kick your high heels off and be more comfortable,' she said. I replied 'I'll be glad to. It's a bind to stand in them for so long.'

'You're telling me!' she laughed.

I'll never forget her genuine compassion for us all.

MRS RUTH PEMBERTON, Prestatyn, Clwyd

When I was a teacher of the hearing-impaired, I felt very excited when I received an invitation to accompany a small group of my deaf pupils to Bridgend Deaf Club, which was to be officially opened by Diana. Unfortunately, not all the pupils were allowed in the actual building, so the younger children had to stay outside in the cold wind.

After the Princess had carried out her official duties, she wandered around the interior of the Deaf Club, stopping by my small group, much to their delight!

Little Lisa – completely uninhibited – took one look at Princess Diana and said, 'You look very beautiful.' Immediately, the Princess replied, 'You are lovely too – and look very smart. I'm going to show you my secret.' To their surprise, she showed the children that she had two safety pins holding the lapels of her jacket in place because of the blustery wind!

As she said good-bye, I asked her if she would do a big favour when she left the Club, and speak to the younger children waiting outside with their flags. She didn't forget, but went straight over to the group and told them how sorry she was to hear there wasn't enough room for them in the building and they'd had to wait outside in the cold.

Thank you Diana, Princess of Wales, for the love, compassion and joy you gave to a group of hearing-impaired children one cold and blustery day in Wales.

MS LYN PEATEY, Bridgend, Glamorgan

December 10th, 1985, the Princess of Wales was to attend a carol concert at Lichfield Cathedral. It was cold, wet and foggy. I reluctantly agreed to take my wife to see her arrive, our daughter joined us at the last minute.

The Princess entered the cathedral, a young glowing girl, in a bright blue velvet suit. She so impressed our daughter, that she asked that we watch her leave.

A car had been parked so that the Princess could step in, thus avoiding the rain. This was ignored, and she went on a walkabout.

The velvet suit was wet but, ever smiling, she shook hands and chatted, gently admonishing someone who had a small child out at, by now, a late hour. She spoke to my wife and, as she shook my hand I have never before or since experienced such a personality, so full of warmth.

CHRISTOPHER GALE, Lichfield, Staffordshire

ॐ

The year was 1985, the date 29 November. My nursing colleague and I ventured into Burgess Hill, West Sussex, when Diana, Princess of Wales was due that morning to open The Ernest Kleinwort Court Home for Young Disabled People. It was pouring continuously with rain and obviously was very bleak and cold. Crowds gathered quickly, but we managed to get to the front of the barrier. Diana came by helicopter, landing in a nearby field and then the rest of the short distance by car.

I shall never forget the moment she stepped out – smiling radiantly as she opened up her umbrella. Her gorgeous long red winter coat certainly brightened up the dull day.

Duty done and exactly a three hour wait for us, her lady-in-waiting following behind, the Princess asked how long we had been waiting in the awful weather conditions and hoped we wouldn't catch cold. She seemed so genuinely concerned.

I suddenly found myself asking if I could see her engagement ring. She laughed and produced her hand, so we all could see. She seemed so very pleased when we all agreed it was such a beautiful piece of jewellery. On her leaving a policeman told us Diana was nearly always late departing – seldom did she keep to time.

I know why – we all do – because so caring, she was and always will be the ordinary people's Princess.

MRS JEAN JAMES, Haywards Heath, West Sussex

On 15 September 1985, by chance, I found myself caught up in the crowds of High Wycombe preparing to welcome the Princess of Wales. Until that time I had been unaware of her visit. My eldest son, Jonathan, four years old, was with me, and whilst I was curious to see the Princess, I was also keen for my son to be able to say that he had seen a member of the Royal Family. As the Royal car approached, excitement built up within the crowd, the Princess stepped from the car and was warmly greeted by applause and cheers. She immediately began conversing with the crowd, taking her time, and shaking as many people by the hand as she could. The bouquets of flowers, all welcome, were collected and passed to her lady-in-waiting. Whilst we were waiting for the Princess to arrive a lady standing next to us in the crowd gave Jonathan a single bloom from her bouquet, she said, 'He must have a flower to give the Princess.' Who would have thought that this single bloom held in the hand of this small boy as he fidgeted in his mother's arms would be noticed in the sea of flowers around him? As the Princess edged her way along the barrier in front of us she suddenly stopped and reached out to take the bloom from Jonathan, saying, 'Is that for me?' He nodded, she held his hand briefly and then moved on taking time to speak to more children, many like my son too young to understand fully who the pretty lady was. As a mother I felt extremely proud that day. Jonathan cannot really remember his meeting with the Princess, but I have in the last few days told him how he once met Diana, Princess of Wales, and how she took the time to acknowledge him as she did with so many people in her short life.

MS ANGELA WEBB, Thame, Oxfordshire

ॐ

In 1985, when I was the Town Mayor of Sandown, Isle of Wight, Princess Diana visited the town to open a new Industrial Estate, to officially name two fire engines after her sons.

Before the event she was introduced to the local dignitaries, who were lined up in a row. As Town Mayor, I was last in the reception line, and as I nervously looked along I noticed that those she was speaking to were all shaking their heads in response.

When she finally reached me, and I was introduced to her by the Lord Lieutenant, she said to me, 'Well, are you going to tell me what the dreadful smell is that is all around?'

'Yes, Ma'am. This industrial estate is built by the sewerage works, which lies just over that hedge opposite!'

She responded with 'Thank goodness someone has told me at last. I was beginning to think it was the Lord Lieutenant's aftershave!'

HEATHER L. HUMBY, Sandown, Isle of Wight

჻

In 1985 Princess Diana came to St. Barnabas, our local hospice. My youngest daughter, then seven, was chosen with a couple of other children to represent her school and meet Princess Diana. It was an awful day, with heavy rain and grey skies. At the time I knew she was due there, the rain was teeming down and as I lived quite near I gathered all the brollies in the house and ran there. The security guard allowed me into the grounds to give out the umbrellas to my daughter, friends and teacher. At the very moment I started to come away, the Princess came out, resplendent in red, smiling at all the smart people waiting to meet her. She looked straight at me and said 'You are absolutely drenched.' All I could manage to stutter was 'It's an honour.' She laughed and said 'I don't have an umbrella either.' And she shook my wet hand. At that point one of her entourage hurriedly appeared with a very large umbrella.

When I got home I caught sight of myself in the mirror – old jeans, soaked baggy jumper, old pair of wellies, looking like a drowned rat! I couldn't believe I had been privileged to be there albeit inadvertently; if it hadn't rained so very hard I would not have been!

MRS LESLEY DIVALL, Worthing, West Sussex

ॐ

I met the Princess of Wales with my daughter Gemma, then aged two, in 1986 at Castleburg Hospital near Settle. When we arrived the crowds were enormous and I thought we would not have a chance to meet her, but through good luck we were standing right in front of her. My daughter had brought a rose from our garden, but by the time she handed it to the Princess it was battered to say the least. I apologized to her for the state of the flower, but she gave me one of those lovely smiles. 'It's lovely, thank you.'

When Gemma and I left Settle that day, we floated home. It is true, as people say, meeting her was a magical experience. Even though this event was eleven years ago, it seems like yesterday to me.

MRS LORRAINE DRAKE, Skipton, Yorkshire

༄

In July 1988, The Princess of Wales was presenting the awards for the Small Business competition that I had organized while I was Features Editor of *Country Living* magazine. It was at the Royal Show in Stoneleigh on a boiling hot day. The tent was stifling and I was nine months pregnant with my first baby. I had not wanted to forgo this meeting just because my baby was due, but the Royal Show organizers were so nervous of an impending birth that they had stationed a St John's Ambulance team right outside the tent. The Princess arrived surrounded by bodyguards with guns bulging in their impeccably cut suit pockets; she looked absolutely gorgeous, though in retrospect I think she was probably quite ill with bulimia at the time. She was certainly incredibly thin, but still stunning, wearing a short skirt, a short sleeve white suit with her long brown legs bare. I am about six inches smaller than she was, and at the time, I was vast with child. She was introduced to me, and instantly said, 'I do want to talk to you about this competition, but I can't have you standing up in that state; you must be exhausted. Come and sit down and we'll chat.' Having had two babies herself a few years before, she must have remembered how it felt to be in that strange, unwieldy, fragile state. I'll never forget the intense cornflower blueness of her eyes, her impeccable skin, her innocent voice. Though I was never a fanatical follower of hers, her thoughtfulness and beauty exceeded every expectation.

KATY BROWN, Shepton Mallet, Somerset

I am a children's book illustrator and had taken a stall in one of the marquees at the Burghley Horse Trials in 1989, shortly after one of my books, *Mouse Mischief*, was published. I had heard that Princess Diana was going to visit and during the afternoon the numbers visiting the marquee were restricted because no one knew exactly when she was going to arrive. I realized that she would probably have time for only a fleeting visit but I still felt optimistic that I would meet her and I signed a copy of *Mouse Mischief* for her to give to her boys as I just had a feeling she would come.

She did. She stopped at my stall and asked if she could buy a picture. I said she was welcome to take it as a gift but she wanted to pay for it. She was ages choosing because she couldn't decide which she liked best and I remember her saying she wished the photographers would go away because the light from their cameras was reflecting off the glass and she couldn't see the pictures properly.

A mouse schoolroom scene was one of my favourites and when I pointed it out to her she said she'd take that. Then she giggled and said, 'This is the worst bit.' She whisked round to her entourage and said, 'Come on then, who's going to lend me five pounds?'

JANE PINKNEY, Keldholme, Kirkbymoorside,
Yorkshire

I met Princess Diana at a charity event in October 1992. All the volunteers were to be introduced to the Princess in groups of 5 or 6. Before Diana arrived we were given instruction on how to address her and so on.

The group I was in comprised four young men and me, a middle-aged woman. The young men were especially excited about meeting the Princess. We all watched out of the corner of our eyes as she moved from group to group and we were pretty keyed up by the time she reached us. When our turn came, Diana gave us such a warm greeting that we all forgot the etiquette we had been instructed in and we just grinned and said, 'Hullo!' as though we were being joined by an old friend that we had not seen for some time. The Princess appeared not to mind at all.

I was happy to stand back and let the young fellows talk with the Princess, and expected her to barely notice me. However, I was most impressed by the fact that she drew me into the conversation and paid as much attention to me, a boring old housewife, as she did the others. I wonder if I would have been that thoughtful at her age if I had been surrounded by adoring men.

I think everyone who ever met Princess Diana was completely captivated by her. Not just her beauty, but by her rare gift of making each person feel special.

MRS MYRA HARMAN, Stondon Massey,
Brentwood, Essex

I was Mayor of Rugby in 1987-88 and it was on the 23 March 1988 that I met the Princess of Wales at the Herbert Gray College in Rugby, headquarters of Relate. We were told by the Chief Executive to stand in certain positions and when we were introduced to the Princess she laughed and said 'You look like The Three Stooges'. I was taken aback at this remark which I had not expected and when she returned from her tour of the College I had to say 'Well maybe so, but were told to be in these positions by the Chief Executive.'

COUNCILLOR REG FRENCH, Rugby,
Warwickshire

ॐ

I had the pleasure of meeting Diana, Princess of Wales on two occasions – one grave, one gay.

The first was when I was escort to the Lady Mayor of Truro, Cornwall, when Princess Diana commissioned H.M.S. Cornwall in Falmouth in 1988.

Lost for many words on meeting her, I did manage to say that the day was lovely, and that she was looking splendid – she was wearing a burgundy jacket and matching skirt. She said 'I know – I look like a Ribena bottle.' We all laughed and were put completely at our ease at once.

The second occasion was a few years later at Treliske Hospital, Truro, when she came down to officially open the Princess of Wales wing to the hospital. I was invited there because I had helped with the fund-raising for a body scanner, and after the opening, she was shown the scanner by two doctors; on coming out, she noticed a small girl of perhaps six years old, waiting for treatment, and who had lost all her hair. She was holding a rose. Diana said 'Is that for me?' and then knelt down to her and picked her up, sat on a chair and put the child on her knee. (Only six people were present.) She cuddled the little girl and told her what a pretty dress she had on. Her mother, sitting opposite, replied, 'Her grandmother made it for her,' and then went on to ask if she might take a photograph. 'Of course,' Diana said. She then turned to an elderly gentleman in a dressing gown who was sitting

46

next to her, and also waiting for treatment. Diana said, 'And how are you today?'

'Much better now, having seen you.' Diana, clutching his hand tightly, said, 'I hope it all goes well for you' and then apologized that she had to go, and took hold of his hand again. Tears fell down his cheeks – and mine as well.

MR ROBERT MALLETT, Truro, Cornwall

࠾

I met Diana when she came to open the children's hospice here in Milton in 1989. She was wearing a bright red suit and as she came out of the marquee to meet us all, someone told her that the suit was covered in talcum powder from sitting on one of the children's beds. She replied that she wasn't bothered by that at all; she had met the children and that was all that she was interested in. A suit could be cleaned.

MRS L. C. TWINN, Milton, Cambridge

☙

I met Diana, Princess of Wales, on a cold March day in 1989. I was a Neonatal Intensive Care nurse and she had come to view the Winnicott Baby Unit at St Mary's Hospital, Paddington, London.

We had, of course, been forewarned of her visit but advised that it was unlikely that she would speak with any of the nurses as her time in the Unit was limited. Just in case, though, we were given instructions on how to address her, should she wish to speak with us.

The Princess arrived on time, looking taller than I expected and very stunning, in a red suit. She was speaking to a mother, when suddenly the alarm went off signalling that the baby was in respiratory arrest, which needed prompt resuscitation. Understandably, the mother was in tears. Diana said a few comforting words to her, and then moved over to my corner. The unit manager explained the baby's condition to the Princess, and then she put out her hand to shake mine, and said, 'Hello. Are you in charge here?' I fumbled a handshake, a small curtsey and a reply, all at once, and then answered a couple of other questions, – when my tongue had become unstuck from the roof of my mouth!

Her final question was, why was the unit so hot? I explained the need for radiant neotherms, to maintain the body temperature of the small babies, and that it did get rather warm for the nurses, though one became used to it in time. Diana then leant forward and whispered confidentially, 'And I'm wearing thermal underwear, too!', at which we both started giggling like schoolgirls together.

After she had left, everyone else was wondering what on earth we had been laughing about and as I was fortunate enough to be the only nurse the Princess spoke with, I shared her secret. We all realized what a down-to-earth and 'normal' person she was, to say such a thing.

Diana was a very special person and she briefly brought a touch of glamour, colour, warmth and humour into our Unit that day and I feel very privileged to have met her. I feel many people feel as I do – that she could have been a friend.

MS ELISE MAHON, London SW14

In 1985, my husband was ill in Cynthia Spencer Hospice, Northampton when Princess Diana came to open the new extension. She sat on his bed, held his hand and talked of her father, Earl Spencer. My family name was mentioned (Spencer) to which Diana said 'There are a lot of us about!' Afterwards, my husband would not let us sit on his bed because he said the lovely Diana had sat there! He came home a week later to pass away, but by his bedside was a photo of the Princess taken on that day. It is still there.

MRS MARGARET WHITTINGTON, Corby,
Northamptonshire

ॐ

My mother and I met Princess Diana in September 1988 at St Catherine's Hospice in Crawley, West Sussex, where my brother, Freddie, aged 34, was a patient suffering from a brain tumour.

Diana took the time to visit every patient in the Hospice and made time with staff and family members of the patients. When she visited Freddie she chose to sit on his bed to speak to us. My brother told her that her visit had come at the wrong time as he was watching the Olympics on TV. Diana responded to this with laughter and replied that her two sons had also got up early that morning to watch the Olympics and she had been rushing about all morning as she was running late. Diana also noticed that Freddie had a copy of *The Sun* newspaper at his bedside and told him not to believe anything they wrote in that paper. She also joked about Arthur, the man in the next bed, whose pyjamas were the same style that Prince Charles wore. Arthur thought this was very amusing.

We will never forget that day. Diana made Freddie feel very special by taking time to talk to him in a human, kind and thoughtful manner and showing that she cared about his illness. This meant a great deal to all of the family, especially to see a smile again on Freddie's face. Diana will never know just how grateful we all were to her for doing that for him.

MRS PATRICIA PUPLETT, Reigate, Surrey

I would like to tell you of an instance concerning my late husband. When he was in St Mary's Hospital, Paddington in 1991, the Princess was paying an unofficial visit to one of her friends, and she also went and sat with my husband, Tony and chatted for about half an hour. This really made him very happy at such a sad time.

Unfortunately, two weeks later he passed away. I was very grateful for her kindness and caring.

MRS M. GARCIA, 144 Empire Road, Perivale, Middx. UB6 7EF

ॐ

I did not have the privilege of meeting Princess Diana, but my mother did. She was at the time in the Maida Vale Hospital, where she was diagnosed as having a tumour on the brain; we had been told that she had only approximately eight weeks to live.

The Princess visited the hospital during the week of 5 June 1987, when my mother, Rose Phillips, was introduced to her. She sat on my mother's bed and held her hand while speaking to her; all my mother could say to us when we visited later in the day was how beautiful and kind she had been to her.

This reflects the person as she will always especially in my heart be remembered.

MRS LINDA GARDNER, London EC1

ॐ

In 1986, our two youngest sons, who were then 6 and 7 years old, were referred to Great Ormond Street Hospital where they were both diagnosed as suffering from Crouzons Syndrome (a craniostenosis deformity). After extensive tests and consultations, surgery was recommended and set for April 1987.

On 13 April of that year Richard, the youngest, was operated on by a team of surgeons led by Mr Barry Jones, who reconstructed his head. Three days later Matthew entered the operating room for a nine hour operation of constructive surgery to his mid-face and nose. This operation was led by Mr David James. During every stage of their stay in hospital I recorded their progress by taking photographs and keeping a detailed diary.

A few days after leaving hospital, we received a telephone call from Mr Jones asking if we would be prepared to return to the hospital for an overnight stay on 6 May, as the Wishing Well Appeal was about to be launched and the hospital were to receive a visit from the Prince and Princess of Wales. They particularly wanted their Royal Highnesses to meet Richard and Matthew, as it was so unusual to have two siblings, so close in age, having such major surgery at the same time.

We returned to Great Ormond Street Hospital and waited in anticipation for the royal visit. During the previous week I had compiled a photograph album detailing our sons' operations and recovery, with a detailed description and I took this album into hospital with me.

Prince Charles and Princess Diana entered the ward and the Princess was guided over to our sons. She spoke to them about their operation and when I asked if she would sign our photograph album she sat down on their bed and looked right through the album reading every entry. The officials who were accompanying the Royal party were concerned about the time this was taking and gently suggested that she move on. She replied that she would make time to see everyone but she wanted to read our book. She then signed the last page, and spoke to us for a few more minutes, before moving on.

The effect that Princess Diana had on our two sons can hardly be expressed in words. They had both gone through a tremendous ordeal. To them it seemed that their reward was the time, attention and care which this beautiful young lady gave to them. It is an experience which has lived with us all throughout the past ten years and our photograph album is still regularly looked at with pride for all that had been accomplished.

On 18 August this year, Richard, who is now 16, once again entered the operating theatre – there have been numerous minor operations in the intervening years – for another major operation to have his face reconstructed. He has made a remarkable and speedy recovery. Just two weeks after his operation, during a follow-up visit to the hospital, we signed the hospital's book of condolences on the tragic death of Diana, Princess of Wales. Richard wrote, 'Thank you. From all your GOSH children all over the world.'

She had touched our hearts and the world will be a poorer place for her leaving it too soon.

MRS JILL ATTFIELD, Dorking, Surrey

I was a patient in the Middlesex Hospital and in the ward there were only two women, myself and one other lady, the rest being men. Princess Diana came in to visit and asked me how I felt about that. I told her it was great as I was unable to get out of bed, so one or other of the men would always bring me my early morning cup of coffee.

She then started to giggle and said, 'I hope none of them walk in their sleep!'

Meeting her was the best tonic in the world.

MRS MARGARET HARPER, Barnet, Hertfordshire

༄

I am so proud of meeting Princess Diana. I was at the Brompton Hospital with my daughter and my day-old grandson. We had almost lost him many times and, of course, were very upset – but I felt I could not show that to my daughter. Then all of a sudden who should walk in but Princess Diana. She went straight to the cot and talked to Anne, my daughter, saying what a lovely baby he was. She asked Anne what his weight was and when she said 'Six pounds, one ounce', Diana said 'Oh, that's when it starts to hurt.' She said 'William was six pounds' and she had hoped he wouldn't be any bigger. Diana said she loved our baby's name, James, it suited him and she wished Anne better, then asked if she could pick him up, and Anne looked at me and I said 'Of course you can.' Diana was so gentle. I had been in tears that morning before I went to the hospital but she made it all right. I asked if I could take a photograph and she said, 'Of course,' and then she asked me if I was the grandmother. She was smiling and giggling with Anne, saying how gorgeous he was and 'I bet Grandma will spoil him.' I said if we got him home he would be spoilt, but he would still be taught not to be rude and Diana really laughed and asked about my other children. She thanked us both and wished Anne well and said 'And I wish you every happiness with your grandson.'

I am writing this with tears in my eyes, not for sadness but for the happiness she brought. I am so grateful that she touched our lives.

MRS ROSEMARY PEARCE, Hockley, Essex

It was 6 June 1991. Princess Diana came to Marlow to open the new baby clinic and my baby daughter, Emma, was chosen to be presented to her because she was such a 'good baby'. We had been instructed on how to curtsey and to address her, but as soon as she walked into the room, I'm afraid all formality and protocol disappeared. I wasn't talking to a Princess, this was just a chat between two mums!

All Diana was interested in was Emma – how old she was, how much she weighed, whether she slept through the night, her names and so on. She was just so natural – no pomp and ceremony at all. She wore very little make-up – and what beautiful eyes. And at that meeting she only had eyes for Emma!

MRS SUSAN HUDSON, Marlow, Buckinghamshire

The story I have to tell is on behalf of my eldest son, Andrew, now aged 6. He was born at St Mary's Hospital, Paddington, London on 22 August 1991. Princess Diana's friend Adrian Ward Jackson was suffering from AIDS at that time and was very close to death, somewhere else in the same building.

The Princess had left her Balmoral summer break to be by his bedside night and day, as she had promised him she would.

During the early hours of the following morning, as a way of trying to console herself, Diana had sneaked quietly into the Lindo Wing nursery – where both her own sons had been born – and where, on this night, just a few babies were sleeping. Andrew was awake and my midwife, Carmen, was giving him a cuddle. The Princess chatted for a bit, then picked up another baby who was crying, sat down, and gave it a bottle. Carmel said she was so relaxed and beautiful and the next morning, she woke me with the words, 'You'll never believe who visited Andrew in the night!'

Everyone has their own story about Princess Diana, but it is very special to us to think that Andrew met her when he was not even 24 hours old.

SUSAN, HUGH and ANDREW PYM. London NW6

ॐ

On 30 April 1993 I was in a road accident and taken initially to Crosshouse Hospital in Kilmarnock, which was closest to the scene, but it was soon discovered that I had a spinal injury and I was transferred immediately to the spinal unit at the Southern General Hospital in Glasgow.

I had only been there a short time when the news was broken to me that I would never walk again. I was only forty years old and had a young son of nine. Obviously, I was devastated. My whole life had been turned upside down and emotionally I was in pieces.

In July of that year I was asked if I would be prepared to be one of the patients being presented to Princess Diana, who would be making a visit to the unit because they were working on a revolutionary new treatment regarding the possibility of re-growth of nerves in the spinal cord. I said I would be delighted. At this time I was lying on a special bed and could not move because my back was broken. I had my left arm in a sling to try to promote some movement.

My bed was taken from the ward to the physiotherapy department where the Princess was to meet a cross-section of patients in different stages of recovery. My bed was placed in a special area sectioned off for bed patients and contained in what I can only describe as a cage, with an opening at the front only.

The atmosphere in the department was electric. My bed was at the very first position where she was to stop.

She arrived. She stepped into my 'area' and I was introduced to her. As there was so little space she stood beside me on her own. She was completely relaxed but still concerned at the same time. She knew what she was talking about and not because she had to. She asked me about my accident and all its ramifications, she asked me about my family, imagined how she would feel in my position. She was compassionate without being patronizing. She was completely genuine and that came across. She did not hurry. She was so serene and relaxed and she transferred these feelings to me. We had a terrific laugh together when she asked about the 'cage'. All through our conversation she had her hand gently laid over mine on the bed. When she finally did leave I had such a wonderful feeling, which she had exuded and filled me with. Only if you met and spent even the shortest of time with her could you understand this. She was exceptional. She always will be.

ANNE M. BALL, Ayr, Scotland

ᢌ

Before I retired I was Secretary of a County Council, and one of my subsidiary tasks was to act as Clerk to the Lord Lieutenant. This involved arranging, with the Palace, all the Royal visits, and being formally presented on each of these occasions. Many involved either the Prince or Princess of Wales, and sometimes both, and I can honestly say that anyone meeting either was always made to feel better for the experience.

In general, I found that despite all the stage managing of the visits, Diana was very much inclined to do her own natural thing, which did not always go down well with some of the guests; by this I mean her wish, for example, to by-pass the VIPs (as they saw themselves) and to speak with those she regarded as her VIPs, such as nurses in hospitals (not the Trustees!), cooks and kitchen staff in schools (not Education Officers and Councillors) and so on.

On one occasion, she was presented with a rocking llama – made locally – by the Mayor, and within a few minutes, he was persuaded by Diana to ride the toy, much to her amusement – and that of the guests, and, to be fair, the Mayor himself.

On another, she was visiting a factory on an industrial estate, and the police were using horses as crowd patrol. As her car turned onto the estate, one of the horses began to relieve itself, and she collapsed into fits of laughter and pointed it out to the protection officers in the car behind. I afterwards learned from her police driver that she also began singing, with her lady-in-waiting, 'She'll be coming round the mountain when she comes'!

But easily the most poignant illustration of her magic with people was on a visit to a new hospice in the county. We had arranged for the Princess to meet some patients, whose lives were very bleak, and she singled out one man who, because of his loss of hair as a result of treatment, refused to remove his hat, so as not to feel embarrassed in front of so many guests.

Following the chat with him, and some five minutes later, Diana was asked to unveil a plaque, and brought a lump to the throat of everyone present by beckoning this man forward, and insisting that he do the formal opening ceremony with her. It was absolutely spontaneous and so appropriate a gesture that everyone present that day will never forget.

WISHES TO BE ANONYMOUS

ॐ

On the day I met Diana, I was pretty nervous. Royal occasions can be exhilarating. They are organized to a high pitch of efficiency, they are often colourful, celebratory – even dramatic; everyone is on their mettle. But they're also daunting, especially to those with duties to perform. This is partly because of the elaborate advance preparations, the official demands for precise timing, the high level of security, the tracker dogs, the extra policemen, the security officers with bulging jackets, the reporters and cameramen, the anxiety that something may go wrong. But it is also more personal. Will I be wearing the right clothes? Not too casual, but not too formal either. Will I remember the protocol, stand in the right place, make the proper form of address, do exactly what I'm there to do? And also, let's face it, will I make a good impression? Will I think of the right thing to say at the right time, will I be quick-witted enough to respond in an appropriate tone, not too familiar, not too sycophantic, to whatever is said to me, or will I, completely over-awed by the occasion and the Presence, be tongue-tied and make a complete fool of myself?

There is also the matter of individual personality. Princess Diana visited the Stratford-upon-Avon headquarters of the Shakespeare Birthplace Trust in 1992 and as the Trust's Chairman I was to receive her on arrival, introduce her to colleagues, and help show her round. I was nervous about getting everything right, but I was also worried about how she might react to me. I am a Professor, and to many people professors as much as princesses can seem intimidating. Diana had often made self-deprecatory remarks about her lack of education, even about her mental capacity. How did she react to professors? Perhaps she would assume I would talk over her head and bore her. None of this contributed to my peace of mind in advance of the occasion.

The visit had been arranged mainly to give her the chance to have a light lunch and a brief pause in a day full of engagements elsewhere. Even so, the town made an occasion of it, decorating the street with banners and laying on a military band. I was at the head of the line-up to receive her at the steps before the main entrance. An area had been cordoned off for the official cars and hundreds of members of the public waited good-naturedly behind the barriers. Security was tight, and we all became rather tense as the time scheduled for her arrival came – and went. Portable phones buzzed, policemen fussed, we chatted nervously and sporadically among ourselves.

As the cars approached, we pulled ourselves together and put on our welcoming faces. Diana stepped out to the sound of applause and greetings shouted by the onlookers, which she acknowledged cheerfully. For-malities were inescapable – the Lord Lieutenant, im-pressively uniformed, had to introduce the Town Clerk, then me, and then I had to introduce the Trust's Director. His taste in ties is, to say the least, colourful and as Diana shook hands with him she leaned forward to peer at his latest adornment, exclaiming 'Wow! What a tie!' The ice was broken.

She looked marvellous – tall, slim, elegant. Above all, she looked relaxed. She glanced observantly around, noticing everything that was going on, but also her big, liquid blue eyes looked straight into those of everyone she spoke to, giving them her full attention, making them feel they were what mattered to her most at that moment. It was not just charm she exuded, though charm was certainly there; it was also con-cern, sincerity, and even tenderness. I began to relax too.

As I led her into the building, she apologized for being late, explaining that she had stayed at a hospice longer than expected. When I said I hoped the visit hadn't been too harrowing, she replied, with unmistakable warmth, 'Oh no, it's something I love to do.' And you knew that it was true, and could see at once how much the warmth of personality she had already displayed would mean to the sick and bedridden.

I took her into the library, where some of the Trust's treasures had been put out for her to see, including a volume with historical material relating to the Spencer family. She obviously knew something about it already, and identified one of the people mentioned there as the black sheep of the family.

As we went upstairs to the room where she was to have lunch, I remembered that a few days previously I had read a news item about Prince Harry having lost one of his milk teeth. It seemed a suitably informal topic of conversation, so I mentioned that the same thing had just happened to my younger daughter, who was about the age of the Prince. Diana laughed. 'Ah, I gather the going rate for the tooth fairy is a pound!' I told her that was rather more than the rate in our house.

After she had had her lunch in private, she met members of the staff, laughing and joking as she did so, and was presented with gifts for herself and the boys before I invited her to sign the visitors' book. One of the photographs taken at the presentation shows her with head thrown back, giggling helplessly in that well-remembered way, at a quip made by the Director. After leaving the building she walked across to the barriers and chatted to the watchers for some time, accepting flowers, before her minders succeeded in tearing her away, and off to the next engagement.

It was a happy occasion, and one that left everybody feeling they had met someone special but approachable. Only a few minutes spent in her company had been enough to convince me that she was very much her own woman and I thought she would be quite wrong to accept and convey a low estimate of her own abilities. I wondered if she really believed some of the things she was reported to have said about herself – as when she toured a hospital laboratory where work was being done on specimens of the human brain and said 'Oh, you wouldn't want my brain!' On the occasion I met her she had displayed an intuitive intelligence, and a quick-witted and immensely sympathetic responsiveness to people and to what was happening around her – qualities worth more than any amount of analytical brilliance.

I was still elated when I got back home and reported on the day to the family.

'Daddy's in love with a Princess,' my daughters mocked.

Well, we all were a bit, weren't we?

PROFESSOR STANLEY WELLS, Gloucestershire.

꒰

I was fortunate enough to meet Princess Diana many times while I was working as a Conference Manager at the Café Royal in London and, on several occasions, escorted her to functions when she was Guest of Honour.

During one event which, as usual, was covered by Press and TV alike, the sheer number of halogen lights used by film crews 'tripped' the fuses and plunged the suite almost into darkness apart from the emergency lighting!

Fearing something more sinister her Royal Protection escorts rushed her out of the suite, and at the door by which I was waiting to escort her out of the building, and to her waiting car almost bumped into her.

Trying to apologize for the incident, I got a beaming smile, a hand extended to shake mine, and the reply, 'Funny, I thought it was time go to bed . . .'

MR FRANCO PACINI, Nuneaton, Warwickshire

౨

My husband has just completed 30 years with the West Midlands Police force, he was a traffic officer and most of his service was as a police motor cyclist. He was a member of the Special Escort Group, here in the Midlands and one of his duties was to escort the Royal Family, members of Parliament and various dignitaries, when visiting the area.

He escorted many, many of these people but the one person who stood out above all others was Princess Diana. It is a very stressful operation, making sure that the car got from A–B safely, many times in adverse weather, keeping to a strict timetable, and always on the lookout for anyone in the crowd who could be a problem. On numerous occasions the person who was being escorted completely ignored the escort team, who, after all, worked very hard to protect them. But the one person who always had a thank you for them was Princess Diana. One occasion which he brought to mind was a cold, rainy day, and the escort group were lined up at the airport. Diana got out of her car, walked across, and shook hands with each officer, thanking them, and my husband was last in the line, and she said to him with such sincerity, 'Thank you for escorting me, and I bet you will be glad to get home to your wife and a nice warm house.'

MRS VALERIE VERNALL, Compton,
Wolverhampton, West Midlands

As Toastmaster at the banquet which followed the presentation of the Freedom of the City of London to Princess Diana, I had to ask the guests to stand to honour her departure. I then led the Princess, escorted by the Lord Mayor, to the door, where I stepped to one side as was routine, and bowed as she and the Lord Mayor passed.

To my absolute delight, she then asked the Lord Mayor to excuse her and came back some yards to shake my hand, thank me by name and did me one of her shy, lovely smiles.

In 43 years of toastmastering only one other Royal has done that – Prince Charles.

BERNARD SULLIVAN, M.B.E. Past President of the Society of London Toastmasters. Petts Wood, Kent

ॐ

When I was on duty as a metropolitan police officer Prince Charles and Princess Diana were frequent visitors to a particular park out of London. On one occasion Prince William, who would then have been three or four years old, had accompanied them. Prince Charles went into the main house and Princess Diana, and William, plus a bodyguard, came into my room. William noticed a packet of sweets opened on the desk. I offered them to him, but Diana said, 'both William and I would love to, but I only allow him sweets once a week and this is not the day.' She then went off elsewhere. When she had gone William dived into the sweet packet and unwrapped at least three sweets and ate them. Shortly afterwards, he and the bodyguard left the room. Diana returned. With William out of sight, she took two sweets and ate them. William came back into the room while Diana was still chewing. Everyone burst into laughter. Diana had a look of such pure innocence on her face which I will never forget and her laugh was so infectious.

MR KEITH ANDERSON, Surbiton, Surrey

I am a tailor with over fifty years experience and I had the privilege of meeting Princess Diana just a few months ago.

It was on the Saturday before the confirmation of Prince William and I was asked by one of my colleagues if I could go with him to Kensington Palace, to advise on the suit that Prince Harry would be wearing for the occasion.

On arriving at the apartments, we were met at the top of the staircase by the Princess. After carrying out all the necessary business formalities, she then arranged for tea to be served to us. She continued to stay on and discuss a number of topics, including her tour of Australia, a country I have visited many times.

In all, she spent approximately an hour and a half with us, which she had no need to do. She was a most charming lady.

MR ARNOLD GRAYSON, Chigwell, Essex

૨

Since 1977 I have been one of seven demonstrating craftsmen working at the Museum of Welsh Life, St Fagan's in Cardiff and during the school half term in the autumn of 1993 Princess Diana and her sons came to the museum on an informal visit.

Within minutes of unlocking the door to the water powered mill that I demonstrate to visitors I had a security man wearing a dark suit at my shoulder asking questions but giving very few answers. About an hour and a half later the man appeared again at the mill, this time with a request that I vacate it of visitors as the Princess of Wales, Prince William and Prince Harry would be arriving within ten minutes. At that moment I had a room full of mothers and schoolchildren, but when I told them who was on the way to the mill I was almost knocked over in the rush for the doorway, as eager mums dragged protesting kids outside to get a good view of the Royal party.

Prince William, walking a little ahead of the party, which included museum management, was the first to cross the mill threshold and by the time the rest were inside the mill he was standing in the centre of the room. Princess Diana immediately noticed that her eldest son and the future king was standing on a trap door. Words of caution were sent to the heir to the throne but he was reluctant to move, despite his mother's request. I said 'Don't worry Ma'am, it's a Welsh trap door, so it won't let Prince William down!' What sounds a silly remark was actually correct, as the trap door in the mill only opens upwards. It broke the ice and from then on there were smiles all round in a relaxed atmosphere.

The royal princes were as curious as all children of their age group to know why there were two ropes, one thin, one stout, passing through the trap door. I invited them to pull for their lives on the thin rope which would answer the question 'What are the ropes for?' After much huffing and puffing their efforts bore fruit and up through the trap door popped a sack full of wheat. The sack continued its journey up through another trap door to disappear into the loft of the mill and there came the sound of vigorous clapping as a proud mother led the way to show appreciation of their efforts in helping the miller in his daily grind. Flushed with their success the princes' next question was 'What will happen to the sack full of wheat now?' I told them that once they had moved on to see another part of the museum I would put the sack of wheat through the wheat cleaning machine to remove the chaff before milling the wheat into flour. 'Can we do that NOW?' the princes asked their mother, but Princess Diana told them it was the miller's decision, not hers, as to whether they could go up into the loft.

I then broke museum rules about letting visitors climb the steep stairway and told the boys to follow me up. Once there, it was all hands to the sack of wheat to drag it to the hopper that fed the wheat into a cleaning machine below. Then before descending the steep stairway I advised my helpers to come down backwards to avoid any mishaps. 'Yes, we don't want any accidents today, do we?' said Prince Harry. After the three of us arrived safely back on the first floor, Prince Harry noticed a Roman quern, whereupon he and his brother tried so hard to turn the whole grains of barley into meal that their industry gave rise to clouds of fine flour dust. Seeing it settle on the boys Princess Diana turned to me. 'If I'd known William and Harry were going to work for you today, I'd have given them old clothes to wear!'

JAMES MARVIN MORGAN, Bridgend, Glamorgan.

ჟ

My son and I had tickets to see David Copperfield at Labatts Theatre at Hammersmith. The show was due to start at 8 o'clock in the evening and had been a sell out for months.

Once the doors opened we all went to take our seats for the start of the show; ours were in the rear row of the left hand block. The show did not start on time, and the audience began to get restless; as the delay grew to half an hour they were becoming distinctly agitated, but nobody came on stage to explain the reason.

Then, after about forty minutes the woman next to me said that the show would soon start now as 'they' had arrived, and she pointed to the next block of seats. I saw the Princess and her two sons taking their seats in the next block. Sure enough the show then began.

Towards the end I went to the toilets. When I returned and went up the stairs to my seat I found that a young lady was also standing there looking over the top of the circle dividing wall to see what was happening on stage; I closed up behind her and looked over her shoulder so I could also see the stage. While I stood there I could see out of the corner of my eye somebody waving at me, I turned to look and saw this large man indicating that I should get back from where I was standing. The lady turned round and I found myself looking directly into the face of Princess Diana. She smiled and asked if she was blocking my view, I said no, and that I was waiting for the illusion to finish so I could return to my seat.

She then said that she was leaving with her boys to avoid causing any more delay and went on to explain that because her car had been delayed they had held up the start of the show and she was worried that many people would be late getting home – in fact, she felt that some might have missed connections already, and for this reason they were going to leave a little early to avoid causing a delay for the rest of the people in the audience.

The illusion on the stage finished and the large man went to fetch the two princes who, because their mother did not want to cause any problems for the rest of the audience, missed one of David Copperfield's best illusions. The party passed me still standing on the stairs and as Princess Diana passed me she said 'Goodnight. Enjoy the rest of the show.'

MR ALAN BURFORD, Hatch End, Middlesex

᪥

At the age of twelve, I was performing in the opera *The Magic Flute* at the Freemasons' Headquarters in Covent Garden. Although I had already sung in sixty-three performances, this was far from the normal occasion, as we had learnt that Diana, Princess of Wales was coming to see the show, and we became very excited at the prospect of meeting her in the line-up afterwards. Before the performance, we took turns to sit in the chair that she was to sit in! The performance itself was the most difficult I have ever sung in, as there was a great temptation to look at the Princess in the middle of each scene, instead of concentrating on the job in hand.

Afterwards we waited for the arrival of the Princess, but I thought that she might pass us by, as we were only children. In fact, she spent more time talking with us than with the adults. She asked me where I had learnt to sing and told me how much she had enjoyed my performance. It meant a great deal to hear her compliment me, and I will never forget it.

SAM BURKEY, West Wickham, Kent

چ

I was lucky enough to meet Diana, Princess of Wales on several occasions over the last fifteen years.

On the first occasion we didn't actually speak. We were at a party given by the Duke and Duchess of Gloucester for Princess Alice's 80th Birthday. I was heavily pregnant with my second child (coincidentally named Harry, and with red hair!) and Princess Diana was pregnant with Prince William (although it had not been made public at the time.) Throughout the evening I kept catching her eye, as she glimpsed my large tummy and we exchanged knowing smiles. She was obviously fascinated by how she was going to look in a few months' time.

The second time we met I was expecting my fourth child, and as we shook hands we joked about me always being pregnant. The following year I met her again in London, and despite not being pregnant and with a new hairstyle she still recognized me and declared laughingly, 'Oh at least you're not expecting this time!' She had just returned from her trip to India where she had been photographed sitting alone in front of the Taj Mahal, and she assured us all that the British press had made a big mistake by reading anything into that, and that she had been admiring the tranquil beauty of the place.

The last time our paths crossed was at another charity luncheon in Birmingham. I was sitting one seat away from her at lunch. She was on great form, very chatty and very giggly; we compared our engagement rings, both sapphires and she jokingly said 'This won't do at all, yours is bigger than mine!' On this occasion I had brought along a photograph of my brother-in-law, Sholto, pictured with the then Lady Diana Spencer aged about ten – as pageboy and bridesmaid at a wedding in Norfolk. She took one look, remembered the occasion instantly and quipped 'I bet Sholto doesn't look as good in tights now!'

During that lunch there was a raffle and several ladies went from table to table to collect money for the tickets. We all dipped into our purses, except, of course, Diana, who seemed rather embarrassed at not carrying any money and blushed slightly. I told her that I would put some in for her and joked that she could pay me later – she laughed and that wonderful Diana smile beamed across her face.

I shall cherish these memories forever; she had the most beautiful blue, almost turquoise eyes and luminescent skin, all of which, combined with her height and wonderful personality, created an aura around her that one would never forget.

THE COUNTESS OF BRADFORD, Woodlands House, Weston-under-Lizard, Shropshire

ᕗ

S everal years ago a young girl in this county died as a result of a brain tumour. Her parents decided to raise enough money for a brain scanner specially designed to detect such cases. Because of their local connections they approached Diana, Princess of Wales to see if she would attend a fund-raising ball.

It was a large and glamorous event and Diana was soon enjoying herself dancing happily with her escorts.

An eightsome reel was announced. Only two sets of eight came onto the floor to perform. I found myself in the Princess's eight. It soon became clear that only she and I (being a Scot and well versed in all Scottish danc-ing) really knew all the steps of the dance, so we found ourselves pushing, and telling the others what to do next. She thought this was great fun and laughed as we con-spired to get the next person to perform their stint in the centre of the eight. I shall always remember the feel of her engagement ring in my hand as we danced when the man between us was taking his turn in the middle and my acute awareness that all the rest of the guests at the ball had gathered to watch us muddle our way through!

It was a memorable evening and as a result of all the fund-raising activities the whole amount of £100,000 was raised on that night.

MRS DIANORA BOND, Southwell,
Nottinghamshire

In September 1988 I was invited to the Royal Festival Hall for a private view of the ballet paintings by Robert Heindel in aid of the English National Ballet of which the Princess was a patron.

As she was surrounded by a crowd of dignitaries and enthusiastic guests, it was impossible for me to get near her either while she was looking at the paintings or afterwards at the reception. At the end of the evening, I bought a print of a Royal Ballet student as a souvenir of the event. As I stood alone in the centre of the room waiting to say good-bye to my hosts, I was very surprised to see the Princess walking towards me, as I thought that she had already left. Noticing my parcel, she asked me if I had bought something from the exhibition. After I had told her what it was, she asked me if she might look at it, not realizing that it was tied up with string. When she saw this, she was most apologetic and held it while I undid it. She looked at it with great interest and asked me if I had any special reason for choosing it. I explained that I had a friend who was a member of staff at the Royal Ballet School and I was delighted when she said that she knew her. We talked for about five minutes by which time a large crowd had gathered around us. She then insisted on helping me to do the parcel up again by putting her finger on the knot.

I shall never forget her wonderful natural friendliness and her rare ability to make one feel uniquely important.

MR GEORGE L. MORGAN, London, W4

I was waiting to enter the Metropole Hotel at the Birmingham NEC, when Princess Diana arrived to attend a charity concert given by the violinist Nigel Kennedy. Without being rushed, she spoke to the handful of people waiting, including me. She was radiant, and as usual most charming, and her eyes made me spellbound. I did manage to utter a few words and to enquire about her children, and she responded very fully, and then enquired about my own family. We shook hands, so I did not wash my hand for sometime afterwards – naturally, my business friends pulled my leg!

It was a great moment, and uplifted me after a very hard day's work at the NEC.

PETER WARRAND, Darlington. Co Durham

ᣒ

I met Diana, Princess of Wales in January 1990 at Champneys Health Farm. The new arrivals were told to meet at 2 o'clock to be shown around and we could not believe our eyes when the Princess walked into the room with two ladies-in-waiting and three bodyguards, all in track suits

My lasting memory of her will be of walking through one of the lounges carrying a pot of tea and a tray of teacups and giggling all the way through the room. I had to pinch myself as I thought 'And this is the next Queen of England!'

I will have this wonderful memory of her, very much alive and happy, which I will always cherish.

MRS SUSAN COOKE, Medbourne, Leicester

ᔓ

My friend and I were at Ascot on Ladies' Day a few years back. We decided to go and look at the horses before the next race when suddenly there was a hustle and bustle about us and we found ourselves face to face with the Princess of Wales. We were absolutely bowled over by her beauty. When we recovered and went on our way, we could not even have said what she was wearing. She did not have to speak, there was an aura around herself which did not need words.

MRS EILEEN J. BRIGGS, Billericay, Essex

ᔥ

Here is my extraordinary experience that I will never forget as long as I live.

I suffer from the eating disorder, anorexia nervosa. For so long such illnesses have been swept under the carpet or even ridiculed. But Princess Diana showed such courage in speaking out that I took strength from that courage.

Two years ago I was very ill in hospital and I wrote to Diana. I don't know why exactly. But it was at a time when the press were hounding her about her illness. I wanted her to know that someone did understand and appreciate her courage. I also wanted to take inspiration from her.

At the most I expected an acknowledgment. I actually got an open, handwritten letter. This came following a phone call. As I was in hospital, my mum took the call and spent twenty minutes talking to the Princess, an entirely natural conversation, covering many topics; she also offered help and support to my mum over my illness. How modest Diana was too. She started by asking if I was there, saying, 'Oh, it's Diana.' So my mother replied, 'Diana who?' Princess Diana finished the conversation with 'I hope I haven't disturbed you'. Didn't she realize it was one of the best events to happen to my mum?

A further surprise was in store for me – an invitation to Kensington Palace. Not only was she kind and helpful, but so natural. We chatted for over an hour;

she had no airs and graces, there was no pomp and ceremony. I was kissed and hugged and told to relax. Her advice and inspiration were invaluable but the whole act in itself was worth more. This busy lady made the effort to spend time with me, to help and also entertain me in her home and not one member of the press knew. It was all for my benefit. I got closer to her than even megastars did, who could merely shake her hand at a function. That she considered me worth all this meant and still means so much to me and my family.

WISHES TO BE ANONYMOUS

༄

The day I met Princess Diana was in March 1997 when I was in a London hospital. I have been suffering from anorexia for many years and was at a very low weight. One of the girls in the Eating Disorders Unit wrote to Princess Diana. She didn't really expect her to have time to visit us with the busy life she had and many other engagements. But she came within a few days to see us.

Having suffered from an eating disorder herself, she understood how we felt. She sat and had a coffee and chatted for an hour to us all, asking us all how we felt about the treatment.

I was lucky enough to sit next to her. We were all very nervous about meeting her but she was so friendly and kind and you felt her warmth as soon as you met her.

Before leaving, she gave us all a book which she said had helped her, and signed it, too. I shall treasure my memories of that day. She just came to visit us all, quite privately. I feel now that I have lost a friend.

WISHES TO BE ANONYMOUS

ॐ

As a GP with an interest in the subject, I was privileged to be present when Princess Diana made her opening speech to the International Conference on Eating Disorders in 1993.

Her audience were all professionals, including many psychiatrists and psychotherapists, and all were startled when, after a deep breath, she opened her speech by saying 'I have it' – followed by a significant pause before continuing 'on very good authority that ...' It was a brilliant touch and everyone I spoke to afterwards was very impressed by the candid manner in which she described her innermost feelings and laid bare her troubled emotions.

All this was printed verbatim in the press and there is no doubt that her courage in publicizing her dis-ease (as she called it) and her strength in overcoming it, gave new hope to her many fellow sufferers.

I had the greatest admiration and respect for her.

DR R. H. LONGTON, Epping, Essex

ᘛ

Diana, Princess of Wales, won a great number of hearts in Zimbabwe. During her trip she made contact with as many charities as possible. Mashambanzou, a small hospice for people with AIDS was one of the places she chose to visit. The Princess requested that there be no media or photographs.

Mashambazou is a home-from-home care unit and takes its name from the Shona 'early dawn' or 'dawn of a new day', the time when elephants (*uzou*) come down to the river to wash and refresh themselves (*kushamba*). The name was chosen for the project in order to offer hope to those on the threshold of a new life.

At 7.30 p.m. Princess Diana was driven through the gates in the dark-green Jaguar of the British High Commission, her personal standard flying. She looked remarkably energetic considering it was early evening and she had been on the go all day. Dressed in a beige suit, drop pearl earrings, flat shoes, she had the casual elegance and style that was special to her.

At the centre she spoke to everyone, lifted up little children who, a little earlier had sung their hearts out for her. Some of the children sat on her knee, one gravely sick little girl stroked her face and pulled her earring. Diana clearly enjoyed the happiness her visit brought to the almost forgotten in our society.

Egipher was no exception. Over the months that she stayed at Mashambanzou I recorded her story as she told it to me. Egipher would visualize herself back in her rural area where the goats and chickens ran about. The old men sat under the shade of a big tree, playing cards. She saw herself fishing in the river near her village ... 'that river is full of fish.' Once she visualized herself eating fruit that had a cure for the virus. She saw herself well and happy as she sat on a blue chair. Then she said, 'I opened my eyes and walked into my room, saw my mother sitting there straight and strong, waiting for me to die, and I felt very depressed again.' A Shona artist painted Egipher in the blue chair and gave it to me in memory of Egipher. Egipher asked me to bring a copy of her story 'in a brown envelope with a yellow ribbon' so I can give it to the Princess.

At about 8.30 p.m. I went to Egipher's bedside with Princess Diana and Sister Margaret, one of two nuns of the 'Little Company of Mary' who run Mashambanzou.

Princess Diana sat on Egipher's bed and held her hand. She asked 'how are you feeling this evening?' One could see how deeply moved the Princess was when the young mother kept saying over and over, 'What will happen to my children?'

Egipher gave her story to the Princess, who asked her if she had written it. Egipher pointed to me saying, 'I did not write it, Liz did, but I told her my story.' Egipher talked about her reflexology treatments and told the Princess what it was like in the rural area where she lived. The Princess explained that she too had reflexology treatments in London and this pleased

Egipher who had been concerned earlier about what she could talk about 'when Princess Diana comes.'

After the Princess left, Egipher remarked, 'Before she came here I wanted to give her my story but I did not think she would be so kind, she seems to understand what it is like to suffer.'

MS LIZ McCLELLAND, Rattingord, Zimbabwe

‿ɔ

Dil Lloyd is an ex Welsh schoolboy international and played centre for Llanelli in his day. In 1993, with England poised to win the Grand Slam, only Wales, in the last game of the season, stood in their way. Dil, in sombre mood, went down to the match at which Diana was guest of honour (as, indeed, she had been on previous occasions). The English lost 10-9, and Wales exploded. After the match, Dil, in company with his wife, had a few drinks at the Angel ... and a few drinks, etc. and eventually climbed aboard the train at Cardiff for the journey back to Reading. Still celebrating, he went along to the train's bar for yet another, and whilst there was told, 'Diana's in the next compartment.' Nothing could restrain him from going to have a peek, only for his way to be barred by two constabulary. Within seconds Dil was laughing and joking with our men in blue, and sharing the day's success. Suddenly, Diana came to join them. 'You lot seem to be enjoying yourselves, may I join you?' Dilwyn totally overcome. 'Ma'am what may I call you?' Diana, 'Please call me Diana, what may I call you?' Dilwyn, 'Please call me Dilwyn – Dilwyn with only one L.' A laughing and joyful celebratory conversation ensued.

Diana chatted all the way with Dil to Reading where he was only too sad to disembark. She autographed his programme, and said 'Goodbye Dilwyn, it has been great to talk to you.' The following day, Dil came into the golf club, still dressed in his red and white scarf, pom-pom hat and all – you have never seen such a devoted fan of the Princess. He would have died for her.

It was this human touch, the ability to connect in with all sorts of people, in a spontaneous and unrecorded way, unrestrained by protocol, that made her what she was. Dil will never forget it.

DAVID HILL, Friend of Dilwyn Lloyd

ॐ

I was working for a security company that collects money from banks, shops etc. It was a sunny mid-week day, around lunchtime and I was taking money to a bank off London's Park Lane. After delivering it, and still wearing my protective headgear – helmet and visor – I marched out of the bank, down the steps and walked across the road, where I had to wait for my driver to turn around further up and then come and collect me.

Just then, a highly polished black car pulled up at the junction, on waiting to enter Park Lane. I could scarcely believe my eyes that sitting in the front was Princess Diana. She spoke to me – or at least, I thought it must be me, after checking behind me to see that there was nobody else in the road. She then spoke again, quite casually – she had her arm resting on the car window, which was right down. She pointed and asked 'What's in the box?' and carried on talking after that, though I can't remember what she said, as I was completely overwhelmed.

I went up to her, helmet still on and money-box in hand, undid the padlock and opened the box and showed her. I said, 'I'm sorry – it's empty.' She smiled, and talked to me again. By this time I was completely blown away. Then, from somewhere deep down, I managed to say, 'Can I shake your Majesty's hand?' She laughed and said, 'Of course you can,' and I took her hand and very cheekily, I kissed it. 'Thank you,' Diana said – and off she went.

I have never felt on such a high as that, ever before. For the rest of the day I was smiling, and feeling the hairs stand up on my neck. I told everyone about it, saying that the papers and television did not do her looks or her personality justice. She actually sparkled – there is no other word for it.

I will never forget that day. She made time to talk to me and I am just honoured that I met her.

WISHES TO BE ANONYMOUS

ॐ

Princess Diana became my Colonel in Chief in 1992, on the formation of a brand new regiment, The Princess of Wales Royal Regiment (Queen's and Royal Hampshires.) I had the privilege of meeting her on a number of occasions but the one I remember particularly was soon after the scandal in the papers of the photographs taken of her secretly whilst working in a gymnasium – much to our disgust.

Shortly afterwards, the Princess visited my battalion while we were on operational tour in Northern Ireland. The norm for such a visit was that each of the companies would put on a display or stand, showing different aspects of our job and it was decided this time that B Company would put on a display of its fitness. I couldn't believe it when we were all marched to the barracks gym to be positioned on various items of exercise equipment. On Diana's arrival, we all had to start exercising.

I distinctly remember thinking how unsympathetic this was, bearing those pictures in mind. But then, when she arrived, and after she had shaken my hand, to my horror the Battalion Photographer started taking pictures! I could not believe it. Luckily someone – I think it was her own bodyguard – mentioned it, and the photographer was quickly moved on. But the Princess was as cool as ever and took no notice at all. This is just one example of how strong she was.

I am currently on operations in Bosnia, where of

course, Diana had only recently visited before her death. I found it very hard to take the fact in. The world is a very much sadder place without her.

SGT. D MILLS, 1st Battalion, the Princess of Wales's Royal Regiment

ॐ

On a glorious Indian summer's day in 1994, we were shopping in Knightsbridge, London. Having walked exhaustively we found ourselves outside San Lorenzo in Beauchamp Place at 1 p.m. and decided to treat ourselves to their excellent pasta and a bottle of wine.

San Lorenzo was renowned as one of Diana's favourite eateries and we wondered whether she might be there on this particular Saturday. We left the restaurant full, but disappointed. Diana had not been there.

We walked past several boutiques when suddenly a dress, the only item in one shop window, caught my wife's eye. We went in and my wife asked to try it on. She descended the spiral staircase joining the tiny entrance to the equally small downstairs area, which housed a dressing room and mirror.

As my wife was changing, two people entered the shop. One was Diana, the other I presume, was her bodyguard.

She was looking naturally beautiful in a T-shirt, denim skirt and flat shoes.

The assistant immediately ran to Diana to greet her and then proceeded to lock the door.

So there we were – Diana, her bodyguard, the shop assistant and me (and, of course, my wife in the changing room, oblivious to the royal shopper).

Diana said 'Hello' to me as she browsed through a rail of designer dresses and finally chose one to try. As she descended the steps towards the changing room, she came face to face with my wife.

'Wow – that's a great dress,' she said to my wife who was now wearing the creation from the window.

As Diana came out of the dressing room with her dress on, she and my wife stood together in the mirror admiring each other. Diana preferred my wife's dress to her own and after much discussion, exchange of jokes and hilarity, they decided to do a swap. They went into the changing room together, exchanged dresses and reappeared, giggling like schoolchildren.

Diana's detective and I were also getting along famously as we dared to comment mischievously on our ladies' attire. After 45 minutes of great fun, we had to leave having decided not to buy the dress. Diana wished us well and thanked my wife for giving her the opportunity to buy the dress – which she then proceeded to do.

We will never forget that special afternoon in London.

RIVA and ANTHONY ULLMANN, Alwoodley,
Leeds, Yorkshire

ॐ

A couple of months or so before Princess Diana's tragic death, I drove my wife Sheila to Harefield Hospital to undergo some medical tests. When we arrived the usual car park was full but because I am a frequent in-patient there myself I know where to park 'round the back.' As I did so, a BMW saloon pulled up behind me and out stepped Princess Diana dressed in a beautiful blue suit and looking absolutely sensational. She had no bodyguards with her nor was there any official from the hospital to greet her. There was no question of this being a publicity mission.

Because there was an immediate atmosphere of informality and friendliness, we each said 'Hello'. She told us that she was on one of her regular visits to comfort a young girl in the children's ward who had been very ill, but before she moved on she asked why Sheila and I were there. We explained my wife's condition and also told her that, coincidentally, I too was a regular patient there to have checks on my 'dodgy' oesophagus. Diana laughed out loud at my use of the word 'dodgy' – she said it was a word that always tickled her. After some discussion about whether our cars ought to be parked where they were, I said if there was any trouble we would go to prison together. She giggled again and went off to the children's ward.

Our return to the car, later, coincided with the Princess approaching her car, ready to leave, still alone. Of course, we were interested to know how the little girl patient was progressing and were pleased when Diana told us she was much improved. Then with the nervous chuckle of someone having been caught out, yet with clear delight and pride too, Diana held out her hands to show what the sick child had done to her. Each finger nail had been painted a different colour – red, blue, green, yellow and black, and Diana loved it! I asked if we might be permitted to shake her hand because we admired her so much. 'Just let me get rid of this', she said, of a folder which she was holding under her arm. She dumped it into the car, returned and not only offered her hand but also inclined her lovely face and did not object when I had the temerity to kiss her gently on the cheek. Then she said, 'I must ask your wife how she got on in out-patients.' And to Sheila, 'Don't bother to get out of the car'; but my wife did and the Princess gave her a warm and caring hug.

Earlier, when Princess Diana had gone into the hospital she had left behind on the seat of her car a fairly large, obvious handbag, so on her return I was bold enough to say 'You are a naughty girl for leaving your handbag on view' and reminded her what the paparazzi would have done if they'd got hold of it. She said if only the media would give to charity some of the vast sums of money they make from photographing her she might not mind so much.

My wife and I were amazed that, although we were respectful to the Princess, we enjoyed a most unexpected familiarity with her – perhaps because of the absence of onlookers. We were also surprised at how much time she was prepared to spend with us under one small umbrella – it was raining a gentle summer rain – as we talked of many things, of her charity work and a great deal about her beloved sons. Throughout our time together she was so down to earth, putting us at ease immediately, so that we felt we were old friends.

My wife Sheila passed away in July, before the tragedy that befell Diana in August, but from the time we waved good-bye to our Princess at Harefield Hospital and until my wife died, Sheila spoke constantly of the charm, the kindness, the humour and the sincerity of a real and wonderful princess – and, dare I say, a friend.

MR RAY HILL, Stevenage, Herts

It was in 1993 that I met Princess Diana. She was visiting the Asian Community Centre in Walthamstow, East London to mark its tenth anniversary. (She and Prince Charles had originally opened the Centre in 1983 when they were still considered as newly-weds.)

What I particularly remember, with much sorrow and tragic irony now, was the comment she made to me as she shook my hand on that day. She had walked over to where I had patiently been standing, when a photographer, who had been standing behind me, decided he was going to push his way past me to capture a photograph of her. On observing this, Princess Diana promptly raised her hand to his camera, very politely asked him to move it away from her face, and then proceeded to take my hand and apologize to me for the photographer's behaviour.

MS L. PHIPPS, London, E11

꒰

It was in early 1990, when my son, then aged six, used to attend swimming lessons at the Cotswold Sports Centre; they were from 8.30–9.00 a.m. When he'd finished his lessons I used to meet him in the shower area, where he had a shower in one of two cubicles; the other was being used. Someone came up behind me and waited a while, then a voice said 'Will he be long?' Without looking back I said 'No'. I then told my son to hurry as people were waiting. 'Don't worry' said the voice behind. I then heard someone say 'Nice to see you Ma'am' and I looked behind me. There stood Princess Diana, a beautiful woman and so tall (I'm only 5'2" and her legs seemed to end at my shoulder). She had a lovely bright pink flowered costume on and bright pink toe nails, and had such a lovely smile. I thought 'Here's Princess Diana, quite happy to wait her turn for a shower!' No 'hurry up and get out' with her. Apparently she used to shower first to go unnoticed into the pool. We watched her swim for a while and she was very good. Being early in the morning, there weren't too many people about but when we left the building later, there, on the wall, were all the reporters waiting, cameras at the ready. I thought then that the poor woman couldn't even have a swim in peace.

MRS RACHEL EDWARDS, Cirencester,
Gloucestershire

I met Diana briefly two years ago, when I worked for a national retailer in Kensington High Street.

Diana was looking for a video for her boys, but was acutely aware that there were tabloid photographers waiting for her outside the shop. She queued to purchase her video, before asking to be ushered out through the rear exit of the shop, to escape the photographers. We were happy to do this for her, and she ran off to her car – the photographers in hot pursuit.

The papers later came in to enquire what she had bought. We followed the usual procedure of 'no comment' – the staff of the store got on very well with Diana, and she trusted our discretion.

In fact, she bought the video of *The Great Escape*. The irony is not lost, in hindsight.

HEATHER WHEILDON, South Cerney, Gloucestershire

ॐ

The day I met Diana was a brilliantly sunny day, but freezing cold.

It was in Swadlincote, near to Burton-on-Trent. I'd said to my husband on the spur of the moment, 'Let's go to "Swad" to see Diana.'

I made up a flask of coffee and off we waited to see our Princess. We stood behind the barriers with other admirers, and my husband said, 'I'd better take my gloves off in case she shakes hands with me.' I replied, 'You'll be lucky.'

When her car drew up, she got out looking a Perfect Princess, and after shaking hands with all the dignitaries, she turned to me and put her hand in mine, and said 'Hello,' and then the same thing to my husband. We were filled with joy and excitement.

In my left hand I was holding a yellow balloon, with 'Imperial Cancer Fund' printed on it.

I've kept it all these years, and today I have watched Diana's funeral with two friends, clutching my precious yellow balloon.

MRS ALICE MANNING, Burton-on-Trent,
Staffordshire

~

My mother died of cancer nine years ago. I was only nine years old at the time and found communicating with my father very difficult.

A couple of month after my mother's death I was assigned a social worker from Barnardo's. She saw that I could not talk about my feelings and knew that she would have to use a different approach with me. So she got me to play a board game, which at the time did not have a name – it is now called 'All About Me' – and this was the turning point for me.

The launch of the board game was in 1992 and shortly afterwards I learned that Princess Diana was to visit Barnardo's in Jesmond and that my father and I were going to meet her. When I did, I presented her with the board game and she asked me a few questions from it and then she told me that when she got home she would play it with William and Harry.

I hope that game will help William and Harry today, as it helped me then.

DONNA WILSON, Whitley Bay, Tyne and Wear

࿇

One day two years ago I was invited to Princess Eugenie's house to play. I had met her once before because my dad taught her mum to fly a helicopter a long time ago. It was a lovely surprise to see Princess Diana and her sons. We all spent the afternoon playing in the garden and in the swimming pool. Then Princess Diana asked me my three wishes. I said to go to Disney World, and huge sweets that last forever in my back garden. It was a lovely day and Princess Diana was a very beautiful lady with a nice personality and she smiled a lot. I wish I could meet her again but she is now in heaven with my dad so she has got the best helicopter pilot in the world to fly her about.

STEPHANIE MULHERN, Steventon, Oxfordshire

༄

Standing at the train station waiting for the 6.30 a.m. train to Waterloo. My thoughts drift over the evening before. I had been unsure about attending this event with my daughter, but I had promised to deliver Mary's lilies and carnations to Buckingham Palace. She is ninety-five years old and past being swept along in a crowd. So here I am, about to embark on keeping that promise.

I recall when Princess Diana visited Byfleet Village to open a Day Centre and how she took the flowers from the little girl I held and asked if she was mine. Her hand extended, waiting for me to take it. In that brief moment time stood still; she looked too good to touch. Her eyes so blue and that sparkling smile. I will never forget her. I promised myself if I ever had the chance again I would take her hand and say something. The chance never came.

And now, here we are. The early morning sun and gentle breeze make it so unreal. These sad occasions are usually on dull, wet, miserable days. Not so today, only the blank drawn faces and predominantly dark clothes bring back the dreadful reality of the coming event.

Our train glides into the station at exactly 6.30 a.m. The journey seems everlasting, stopping at various stations to pick up more unhappy people. We note the empty carriages going north. All the people are heading south, converging on the capital.

As we get off the train at Waterloo, dark clothed

people appear from every carriage, all moving silently towards the exit. Showing our tickets we pass through into Waterloo Central Station. No queue for coffee or the cloakroom. Where are all the vast crowds?

We follow a small trickle of people leaving the station, all moving silently in one direction, over Waterloo Bridge. Big Ben looms up, and the Houses of Parliament bathed in sunshine. Despite the crowd becoming more intense the silence remains. Then, as we turn into Westminster we are confronted by a huge crowd of people.

It was such a strange sight, bodies lying by walls, still in sleeping bags, candles flickering, cups of tea being made, all here in Westminster. Yet in all this a small pathway had been left by the mass of bodies, so people could pass through. It was like going through a field of corn, except these were people. All wanted to help each other with such an unusual need to be respectful and kind.

Approaching the Mall we found the crowd had thinned out. This is where we would stop to pay our respects to Princess Diana. Taking note of our companions who will share our emotions and thoughts with over the next few hours. Complete strangers all brought together by the same need.

Across the road an elderly couple were fast asleep in garden chairs. A young man decided to dance around with feathers and flowers attached to his head, vibrant colours, pink, yellow and green. Shouting incomprehensible sounds while policemen keep an eye on him. Our group are anxious, wanting him to be caught before the procession arrives; then suddenly he disappears and we can breathe again. Two young girls behind us are discussing Diana's obvious beauty while reading the newspaper and an older couple are giving a running commentary on the arrangements that are taking place.

We hear the horses coming and the gentle rumble of the gun carriage, complete silence falls and the only movement is of the leaves occasionally dropping from the trees. Soon the dreadful truth will be before my eyes but I don't want to believe it. People start to shuffle and weep and our grief is increased when we see Princes William and Harry bravely walking behind their mother's coffin. It's difficult to imagine the extent of the intense pain and anxiety they must be going through. To behave in such a strong and dignified way, while the public weep and wail – where does that kind of strength come from in ones so young? I avert my eyes, feeling like an intruder.

We collapse in heaps of misery and try to make sense of what we have seen, but it makes no sense. We sit in the park watching the toddlers running around, every now and then sending birds fluttering into the sky to the tune of 'Candle in the Wind'.

With the service over, we make our way to Buckingham Palace to lay our flowers. I place them by the lions. Mary would like that. She has campaigned all her life for animal rights and humanitarian causes, so what better place to put them? The floral tributes are beyond belief. Vast carpets of fragrant flowers stretch out.

As we return to the station strange sights greet us. Bunches of flowers lie on the grass where people had stood listening to the service; candles are still flickering in odd places. The crowds have dispersed leaving newspapers everywhere – Diana's face staring up at you.

It's 1.30 p.m. and already the special tribute papers are out on sale. As we pass over the bridge to enter the railway station a military vehicle, accompanied by a police escort, passes beneath us. The breeze has blown the khaki cover up on a corner revealing the empty gun carriage.

The finality of it came home then, the saddest moment of all.

MS ANN HARRISON, Sompting, West Sussex

༄

L ate at night. Crowd outside the Coliseum, London. The lady beside me held a posy.

Down the steps she came. The crowd sighed. She ignored her car – crossed the road.

'Are these for me?' And she smiled.

I forgot the camera ready in my hand, and just watched her out of sight.

SUZANNE SAINSBURY, Plymstock,
Plymouth, Devon

❧